How

A

Sandra Ashman and Phyllis Creme

University of North London

How to Write Essays

Sandra Ashman & Phyllis Creme

1st edition 1980

2nd revised edition 1990

3rd edition 1992

Reprinted 1993

This edition 1996

ISBN 1 85377 137 6

University of North London

166-220 Holloway Road, London N7 8DB

The University of North London is a Charity and a Company Limited by Guarantee. Registered in England No. 1000834.

Contents

1
Approaching the Essay

As a student you will almost certainly have to produce essays during your course. Some will be written during term time and contribute to course work assessment, others will be answers to questions set in formal examinations. An essay is usually defined as a continuous piece of writing ranging in length from at least 500 words to about 5,000 words for a special or extended essay. But this booklet is not just about 'writing' essays, it's about the various stages you need to consider when producing an essay and about the ways in which producing an essay helps you to learn. The time given to each of these stages will of course vary according to the conditions surrounding any particular essay. Let's look at the first stage - which is approaching the essay.

Why write essays?

If we understand the value of doing something, it usually helps to make us feel more positive and confident about the task. So what is the value of writing an essay? Here are some ideas - you might think of more. It forces you to organise your own thinking and develop your own point of view on issues. In one sense, writing is the crucial step which helps you get to grips with new ideas and new experiences. Without that step, it's very difficult or impossible to know how much you've really understood.

Expressing yourself - ideas, new information, or whatever, in written form, really is a life skill - which you will need in almost every area of work. Essay writing gives you practice and develops that skill. If it's a term time essay, you can see it as giving you practice for writing under exam conditions. And don't forget that the essay provides very useful revision material.

Lastly, it gives you a chance to get feedback from your tutor about their assessment of how much you've understood and how well you are able to communicate this. With your tutor's help, you can identify areas of strength and weakness so you know where to concentrate your energies next time. So, approach your essay positively. It can be a very valuable learning opportunity.

Course conventions?

Of course, you must also check out any particular requirements your course or department might have for that particular essay. How long should it be? Should it be presented in a particular way - typed, for example? If you know the answers to these questions, it will help you to feel more confident about the task.

Written versus spoken

One last point in this preliminary stage is to remember that there is a difference between written and spoken communication. You must select your words more carefully and make your meaning absolutely clear. Remember you won't be beside your reader to explain any difficult or obscure points. It's more important too, to have a sequence of logical steps so that your reader can follow your train of thought. Any emphasis has to be conveyed through vocabulary, sentence rhythm or punctuation. And because your reader can go at his own pace, even go back, if necessary, writing can be much more concentrated than speech.

All this has been about the general framework in which you approach your essay. Now we'll go to the next stage which is to examine the task.

2
What is the Question?

Understanding the question

You need to examine the precise wording of the question, in order to decide exactly what you are being asked to do. You will also need to consider the assumptions behind the question and the implications that arise from the question's statement or assumptions. Does the topic require general treatment or specific reference to certain aspects? Are your own experiences and opinions worth expressing - or should you refer only to the knowledge of others?

Key words

It is often useful at this stage to underline what you think are the key words in the way in which the question is worded. Look for the vital words or phrases which will determine the style and structure of the answer you will write. A list of the key directive words frequently found in essay titles is given below and this might help you understand what is being asked of you in an assignment.

Some terms frequently used in essay questions:

Compare

Look for similarities and differences between; perhaps reach a conclusion about which is preferable.

Contrast

Set in opposition in order to bring out differences.

Criticise

Give your judgement about the merit of theories or opinions or about the truth of facts; back your judgement by a discussion of evidence or reasoning involved.

Define
Set down the precise meaning of a word or phrase. In some cases it may be necessary or desirable to examine different possible or often used definitions.
Describe
Give a detailed or graphic account of.
Discuss
Investigate or examine by argument; sift and debate; give reasons for and against. Also examine the implications.
Evaluate
Make an appraisal of the worth of something, in the light of its truth or usefulness. Include, to a lesser degree, your personal opinion.
Explain
Make plain; interpret and account for; give reasons for.
Illustrate
Use a figure or diagram to explain or clarify, or make clear by the use of concrete examples.
Interpret
Expound the meaning of; make clear and explicit, usually giving your own judgement also.
Justify
Show adequate grounds for decisions or conclusions; answer the main objections likely to made to them.
Outline
Give the main features, or general principles, of a subject, omitting minor details and emphasising structure and arrangement.
Relate
(a) Narrate - more usual in examinations.
(b) Show how things are connected to each other, and to what extent they are alike, or affect each other.
Review
Make a survey of, examining the subject carefully.
State
Present in a brief, clear form.

Summarise
Give a concise account of the chief points of a matter, omitting details and examples.

Trace
Follow the development or history of a topic from some point of origin.

Scope of the question
Two other points to note: you will need to see how many parts there are to the question and what weight you will need to give to each. And what are the limits of the topic? It is very important at this stage to realise that you are not embarking upon a piece of open-ended research. You must be rigorously selective both in your approach to collecting material and to the writing up - choosing only material that is relevant to the answering of this question.

Ask
Remember - if you're still unsure, you have other sources who might be able to help. Your student colleagues might also find it useful to discuss exactly what the question requires. If you're still in doubt, ask your tutor. After all, s/he set the question and won't be keen to see you waste a lot of valuable time through misunderstanding. Once you feel confident that you understand what is required of you, you're ready to move on to the third stage, collecting the material.

3
Collecting the Material

Of course, it's important to collect material that is relevant. But how do you go about that? It's all too easy to pick up a pile of books that look vaguely useful and browse amongst them. This might be fun - and you might learn something, too. But it won't help you get your essay written.

It does often help, though, to quickly jot down at this stage what you do know about the question. It's probably more than you realise and it will help get your subconscious mind ticking away on the subject. It might also give you certain 'leads' to follow up.

Questions - purposeful reading

You must read purposefully and systematically and in order to do that, you'll need to formulate a set of questions before you start to read. Examine the essay topic again and write down a few questions which you need answers to, if you're going to cover it. As you read, more specific questions will come up - and you can look for answers to these, too. There's a limit to how much research you can do for any piece of writing, so make sure you're finding answers to the main questions first.

Start early

It is a very good idea to start early. Do some preliminary thinking and formulate a few questions as soon as possible after you have heard the title of your essay. This helps you avoid that last-minute panic and should allow time for reviewing and revising your first draft.

There are other reasons for starting early. You might miss useful ideas that come up in your reading or in discussion - or just listening to the radio - if you don't see their significance. Have you ever noticed how often you hear a new word once you've bothered to check its meaning and understand it? We note new ideas only when we have some framework which allows us to see their significance. If you're really thinking hard about your question, it's also likely that your subconscious mind will go on working on it and you might find you see new relationships between ideas.

A variety of sources

A major source of ideas and information will be the booklist provided by your tutor - you can take this further by checking the bibliographies of the books on this general booklist and see if they can indicate further useful sources. Similarly, use encyclopedias, research papers, journals, government material. Your own notes, from lectures and other reading, might also provide useful material. But don't ignore other sources - ideas can crop up in lectures, in discussions with friends, in newspapers and magazines - or in a TV programme.

Keep a notebook

Use any source available to you - it's useful to keep a notebook with you to jot down ideas, quotations, or examples as you come across them. If you need to, you can always follow them up later. If you don't record them, you'll almost certainly forget a lot of them. Or else, your mind will be so cluttered up, trying to hand on to every small point, that you'll have no time for more creative thinking. As an alternative to a notebook, some students prefer to use 8" x 5" index cards which can be easily 'sorted' and 'shuffled' when you come to plan your essay. Try this technique on one of your essays and see if it suits you. If you are lucky enough to have access to a wordprocessor, of course, you can sort and shuffle your information more easily than by using index cards. But don't forget to make a back-up!

Record the sources

You'll have to record all the sources you use and you could perhaps keep this information in your notebook too. Write down the title and author if it is a book, or the name of the speaker. Remember you must give credit to these sources - it might just be a short booklist at the end of your essay.

Don't plagiarise

If you use direct quotations, however, you must put in a footnote with a precise reference to the source of that quotation. Using other people's work in any acceptable way does pose difficulties sometimes. It does help a lot if you always take notes in your own words, and this also helps you to check your own understanding of a topic. But remember, plagiarism, which is using other authors' words without acknowledgement, is something you must avoid when writing your essay. Not only is it unacceptable and a 'literary theft' but it will unbalance your essay. Nor do you want too many acknowledged quotations. Only use those phrases or sections which are so telling that no paraphrase of the author's idea will be as effective.

Once you have most of your material in note form, you are ready to start planning the essay outline, which is the fourth stage.

4
Planning the Essay Outline

The importance of planning

Planning an outline for your essay gives you a basic structure from which to work. It helps you sort out the main ideas and the important details you will need to explain or illustrate or develop these ideas. It also reduces the risk of leaving out some really important fact or argument.

You will probably find the writing of your essay much easier if you are working to a plan. The reader will probably find it easier to follow because your writing will be more fluent. Another point to remember is that in an exam, if you are short of time, a clear outline will earn you more marks than a half-finished essay. Of course, you should never be so rigid that you can't move away from your outline. Perhaps some new idea or relationship has only just occurred to you and you need to reorganise your material to include it. But be very careful that it really is useful material for your argument and not just irrelevant padding.

Selecting the material

Selecting the main points and allowing enough space to develop and illustrate them is often seen as the most difficult part of tackling an essay. Going carefully through each step in stages two and three will help - particularly, collecting material that is relevant to the questions that you have formulated about the essay topic. It is often painful to discard material that has taken some time to assemble, but it is never a good idea to include all your material just because it's there. Think hard about the relevance of it to your main points - this is how a plan can really help you. Some people find that keeping their notes on index cards helps them in this sorting out and selection part of the job; others use just one side of the paper for their notes and then cut them up and organise them. It might seem expensive on trees (if this worries you - use recycled paper), but it will probably save you time!

The advantages of owning or having access to a wordprocessor when writing essays are immense: you can move material about, put to one side, or try out different ways of ordering it. But don't forget to keep a back-up copy.

A basic framework

You've probably been told that an essay should include the following three parts:

Introduction
Body of the essay
Conclusion

But it is probably worthwhile just considering what is meant by these.

The introduction should contain some comment on the topic of the essay - perhaps definitions are needed, or some explanation of what you understand by the title. This section should also state which aspects of the topic you intend dealing with and why. Remember you are not writing a book - so you'll be selecting the three or four main arguments that support your answer to this particular question. Your introduction thus directs the reader - giving him a clear idea of what is to follow.

The body of the essay will take each of these main points and develop them with examples and illustrations. Later in this booklet you can read about how to use paragraphs and sentence structure to deal with these main ideas and supporting evidence.

Your conclusion will summarise your main ideas. It might also be appropriate to give a firm or tentative answer to the question. Or you may have chosen a question where you need to suggest the wider implications, or future trends. Or suggest to the reader areas worthy of further consideration. It is in this section that you can introduce your own views - as long as they are based on the arguments that you have developed earlier.

If it helps to have some idea of the length of each section, the following is a very rough guide - not a regulation.

Introduction	**7-8% of total length**
Conclusion	**12-15% of total length**

Other ways of planning

You will of course be experimenting with ways of planning your essays to find a method that suits you. Some other ways that might be worth thinking about are mentioned in this section.

Have you heard of 'pattern notes'? This is a method that can be used either for taking notes or planning ideas, and it was developed by Tony Buzan. Rather than starting from the top and working down in sentences or lists, one starts from the centre or main idea and branches out as dictated by the individual ideas and general form of the central theme. Buzan argues that the brain does not work in a linear manner and that conventional ways of taking notes or planning are therefore not the most useful. If the brain works with key concepts in an interlinked and integrated manner, it makes sense to structure our notes and our word relations in this way, rather than in the traditional 'lines'. The diagram below is an example of pattern notes, which is simply, in this case, jotting down initial ideas around a centre and drawing in links between ideas.

Many students have found this way of working very fruitful and it can be a very creative way of working - since the mind should be left as free as possible, noting down quickly every idea your mind generates around the central idea. Once the pattern is completed, all the information is readily available and all that is needed is a decision as to the final order in which to present the information. Buzan claims that students using these techniques at Oxford University were able to complete essays in one third their previous time while receiving higher marks.

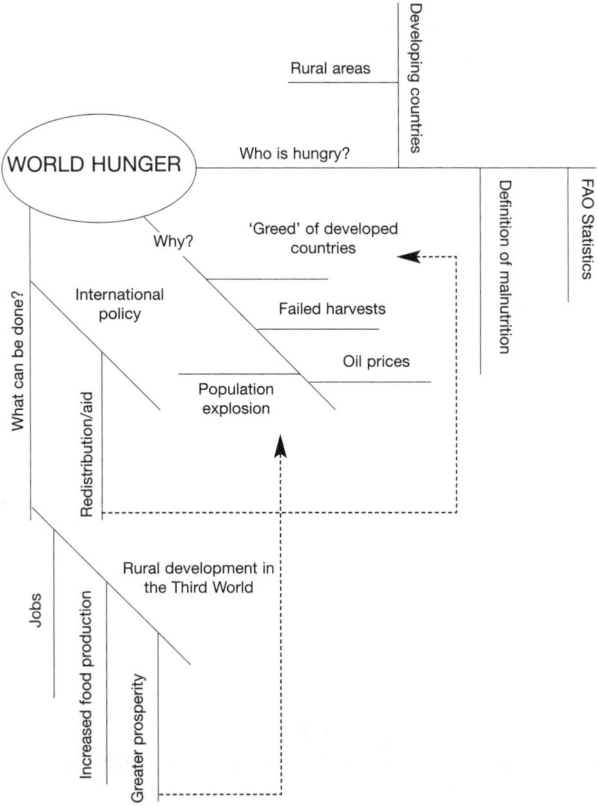

Essay Title: Discuss some of the causes of world malnutrition and discuss possible solutions

If you would like to read more about Buzan's ideas, look at his book Use Your Head, particularly Chapter 5, 'Brain patterns - for recall and creative thinking' and Chapter 6, 'Brain patterns - advanced methods and uses'. You could also look at the programmes which accompany these chapters and which are available on video.

Some students find that writing the last paragraph before they even start the essay is a useful technique. It gives direction to the essay and makes sure that there is a firm conclusion - rather than a petering out as you run out of ideas.

Always plan

Remember that planning may take a few minutes (as in an examination) or much more time may be spent on looking for information and ideas and in discussion and thought. But however much there is available, the first steps must be to organise your thoughts and to draw up a plan. Only by preparing a plan can you maintain control of your material and present your subject in a logical, concise and coherent way.

5
Writing the Essay

At last we've reached the stage that some people think is where essays start. But it's a much easier stage if you've followed all the earlier suggestions. If at all possible, write a first draft, when you don't need to worry about precise wording. Follow your plan and get all your ideas down. Ideally, you should then leave your draft for a few days, so that you can review it a little more objectively. It's very easy to be so delighted to have produced something - anything - that powers of self-criticism become blunted.

Style

Many students worry about their writing style but remember your words express your thoughts and if you've got a clear plan and a real grasp of the material then you will have very little trouble writing with clarity and coherence. It's much better to use simple and straightforward language, although there is the difference between written and spoken language that was mentioned earlier. That doesn't mean you should use obscure or complex words and phrases - merely that you must avoid slang and abbreviations and any reliance on the other forms of communication we can use when we speak. Generally, stick to short sentences, although a counsel of perfection might be to vary these with longer sentences occasionally. But the main objective is to be clear and concise so that your reader can follow your argument easily and is not distracted (or irritated) by irrelevant padding.

Layout

Once you have introduced your subject, you must decide which is the topic for each paragraph. Your plan will guide you here but you must now decide in detail:

What diagrams are needed and where should they be placed?
How can the paragraphs be best arranged in logical sequence?
Would sub-headings help the reader?

Paragraphs

Whilst you intend that the ideas in your essay should add up to some overall statement, you must also ensure that each paragraph has unity and should link naturally with preceding and following paragraphs.

A paragraph normally deals with one topic or aspect - it may raise a central issue, or it may develop that idea. Or two paragraphs may be on different topics but linked by that difference - you may have two paragraphs dealing with cause and effect, or positive and negative aspects of one argument, or before and after. Often, the first sentence of the paragraph is the topic sentence - that is, it explains what the paragraph is about, it gives the main theme for the paragraph.

Transition

The transition from paragraph to paragraph often presents some difficulty - but it is essential to maintain continuity and to give verbal signposts to your reader showing how you are moving on. Some common linking words and phrases are:

but, however, on the other hand, yet
indicating contrast;
for example, that is
indicating illustration;
similarly, moreover, furthermore, in addition
indicating extension;
therefore, consequently, as a result, thus
indicating conclusion;
then, after that, ultimately
indicating the next step.

Booklists

At the end of your essay, you should give a simple list of the publications you have consulted. If appropriate, also list the people and organisations you have contacted. This is useful to the reader, and also later to you when you might wish to check back on certain points - or expand and take further some of your ideas.

The review

As mentioned earlier, a review is very useful even though it may not result in much rewriting. You might even get a friend to listen while you read aloud - this can help a lot if you are worried about clumsy sentence structure or illogical ordering of your ideas. If you've no willing friend with time to spare, try tape-recording your read-through and listen to yourself as critically and objectively as possible.

A review checklist

Here's a review checklist which might be useful for you to see if you have gone through all the necessary processes in the preparation of your essay.

- **Have I answered the particular question that was set?**
- **Have I divided up the question into separate smaller questions and answered these?**
- **Have I covered all the main aspects?**
- **Have I covered these in enough depth?**
- **Is the content relevant?**
- **Is the content accurate?**
- **Have I arranged the material logically?**
- **Does the essay move smoothly from one section to the next, from paragraph to paragraph?**
- **Is each main point supported by examples and argument?**
- **Have I acknowledged all sources and references?**
- **Have I distinguished clearly between my own**

ideas and those of others?
- **Is the essay the right length - both according to the word limit set and for its own purpose?**
- **Have I written plainly and simply?**
- **Have I read it aloud to sort out clumsy and muddled phrasing?**
- **Are the grammar, punctuation and spelling acceptable?**
- **Is the essay neatly and legibly written?**
- **Have I presented a convincing case which I could justify in a discussion?**

Appearance

Finally, now is the time to consider the appearance of your essay. Is it clearly written - or typed/wordprocessed? Does it look well laid out? First impressions are important - however unfair it may seem, there is an element of subjectivity in essay marking. It's a pity to drop even one grade on your mark because of something so easy to rectify as presentation. If you're really well organised, it may be worth keeping a second copy (a carbon copy or photocopy). Essays have been known to go astray between you and the lecturer.

The last section is perhaps the most often neglected - and yet it is vitally important to you.

6
Learning from the Essay

You will have already learnt a great deal about the topic of your essay and something of peripheral issues through your research and thinking. In writing the essay, you will have consolidated this learning. Once the essay is returned to you by your tutor, you can use his or her comments for further learning.

S/he might, for example, suggest new ideas, fresh examples, different opinions. All of these will be worth considering whilst your arguments are still quite fresh in your mind.

Of course, there may be simple corrections of facts, or mistakes. Note these! There may be comments concerned with your writing style - suggesting how you can express yourself more clearly - or remarks about the detailed aspects of the structure of your essay. Study all these carefully.

The overall comment you receive will evaluate your essay as a whole, and probably involve some justification of the mark you receive. Your tutor will give some thought to these comments so that they are as useful to you as possible. S/he may refer to earlier work you've done - or mention difficulties you might encounter in work to come. All of these are opportunities for you to learn from all the work you have already invested in your essay. Don't waste them.

These comments from your tutor may come in a written form on your essay - which is a very good reason for leaving plenty of space for this sort of feedback, in margins and double spacing, or by using one side of the page only.

Or you might have the opportunity in a tutorial for a longer discussion - in which you can clarify for yourself and develop the meaning of some of the comments made.

The last resource available to you, and generally the most under-used, is your fellow students. Why not exchange essays and learn from each other? Students who have tried this have found it to be of real value. All too many of us have experienced that feeling of anticlimax after investing a great deal of thought and energy in some task - only to receive no reaction or feedback from anyone. Learning in Higher Education is about using all the resources around you to the full.

It must be clear to you by now that essays are about a lot more than just covering four to six sides of A4. They are a vital part of your learning and it's up to you to maximise their usefulness to you. Enjoy your essays...

Other Study Guides available from Blackwell Bookshops:

Taking Notes from Lectures

Your notepad's out, your pen's at the ready, but can you convert the stream of words you hear into a form that will be of use to you afterwards? How often have you turned back to old lecture notes to discover a mass of unconnected phrases whose importance you can no longer remember? This handy pocket guide gives clear, concise advice on what to look for in lectures, and how to put it down efficiently for easy recall and revision.

Reading for Study

Are you reading effectively? For most students, reading is so automatic that you may not recognise it as a skill - and a skill that can be improved. Do you really get the best out of your books? Is your reading helping you as much as you would like? Do you wish you could read faster? This guide shows you how to improve your capacity to read for study, showing you how to adapt the way you read to the task in hand. Read it - you'd be surprised at what you could learn...